DESIGN MANAGEMENT for SMEs

DESIGN TOOLS FOR MAKING BUSINESS

Not only start-ups.
Innovation through existing European micro, small and medium companies. Business opportunities through incremental innovation and design thinking.

*Curiosity is the spice of life.
Who is not curious stands still, satiated with himself.*

ALESSANDRO BARISON

DESIGN MANAGEMENT
for SMEs

DESIGN TOOLS FOR MAKING BUSINESS

This text is self published by abitudinicreative.it.
©2014-2015 abitudinicreative.com

abitudinicreative ® is a registered trademark.
abitudinicreative is a project by Alessandro Barison.

The contents of this text are protected by copyright and may be used for non-commercial works quoting the source: abitudinicreative.it.

In this text I used citations and images of public domain, underlining, where possible, the source. If case of errors and / or omissions verified by the legitimate owners of the copyright, the author is available for the appropriate corrections.

If not specified otherwise, pictures contained in this text are property of the author.

All trademarks mentioned are the property of their owners.

This text tells the author's point of view only.
The blog abituinicreative.it is not an editorial product, as it is not updated on a regular basis.

INDEX of CONTENTS

Nice to meet you.

Preface.

Product Design.

Design Thinking.

Creative tools.

Design Management:

- Protagonists and interlocutors.
- Tools.
- Methods.
- Brand Awareness and identity.
- Corporate structure.
- Be known and be informed.
- Foresight and storytelling.

Workplace Design.

Strategic design.

Brand reputation, web and social networks.

Corporate social responsibility.

The future is now.

Bibliography and sitography.

Thanks.

About me.

Nice to meet you.

Design is a buzzword, more and more often confused with other words such as style and invention. We forget that design means first of all project. In companies, particularly in small and micro companies, to decline the culture of design in all business activities is a rarity. With the driving force of design it's however possible to enhance the company's resources and create opportunities for unexpected growth. Design Management is the new challenge for designers and entrepreneurs in the beginning of this millennium. My experience as an entrepreneur and designer is narrated in the following pages, dedicated to small businessmen and young designers.

Writing is good for everyone, teaches how to communicate, first with yourself.
With these words, received by e-mail on a cold December day, some years ago, I decided to collect my notes in a structured text, certainly useful to remind myself what has been done and what remains to be done, a text possibly useful to those who read me, a motivating journey, a trace of discussion on the urgent need to do business and make creativity works with a new point of view, different from the past. The contemporary economic and financial difficulties, from

many points of view, is a danger, but also an opportunity, especially for small companies and young designers, that in these situations often have on their side the ability to change more quickly and a higher dynamism compared to large companies and old designers. In the next pages I will try to describe my experience as entrepreneur and designer, my personal adventure into the world of small companies and creativity, an adventure characterized by difficulties, mistakes, fatigue, but also stubbornness, satisfaction and results.

This text is the result of the work, the study and the research that I carried out from 2006 to 2013, in particular summarizes my curriculum at the design school Scuola Italiana Design; my work at the Design Management project for my office furniture company, Emme Italia, which got an Honorable Mention for Micro Companies category during the Design Management Europe AWARDS ceremony, in 2009; the research for the blog abitudinicreative.it and designforyou.it; the collaboration with Schools and Institutions on educational projects of Design Management, Brand Design and Marketing for SMEs.

Alessandro Barison.

Preface.

A recent report for the European Commission is the confirmation that SMEs are the backbone of the European economy. In Europe, 90% of companies are SMEs, more than 60% of employment is in SMEs, also, 90% of European SMEs are micro enterprise. SMEs generate more than 50% of European Global Value Added, but are often forgotten in favor of large companies. Existing SMEs are interesting opportunities for European growth, with a huge innovation potential, but the attention of media and public institutions is unfortunately focused quite only on start-ups and high technology projects.

Innovation is easy in a new start-up, but it's a difficult puzzle for existing SMEs. The management of pure innovation and high technology projects is very heavy, the management of incremental innovation systems is lighter and more effective in SMEs. The key to growth for European SMEs is the adoption of processes of incremental innovation and a shift from the management of individual projects to the systemic management of the company's overall potential. In order to be competitive in this beginning of millennium, are no longer enough to realize good individual projects. You need an innovative holistic approach, involving, step by step, all aspects of your business.

To give back competitiveness to SMEs is necessary to rethink the structure management of companies. New projects must move the focus from the particular to the general, from the contingent needs to the strategy, from the pure innovation to the incremental innovation. Individual projects must not be abandoned, but should be rethought in a more holistic, consistent and comprehensive system.

While maintaining the traditional project management actions, SMEs have to activate new processes of system management, involving new and more numerous players, new, larger and more complex areas of intervention, new skills, new goals.

The integration of the project management with the system management, implemented thanks to the tools of design management, allows you to enhance the potential of SMEs and to give competitiveness in a market like today's, which quickly moves from the pure consumerism to conscious consumerism.

To activate a process of design management in a SME is first of all needed a change of perspective and mindset. Design Management has new keywords and new interpretations of existing priorities. SMEs that want to look to the future with foresight must be ready for a long and difficult process of analysis, research, and redesign of the entire corporate structure.

Design Management does not destroy the tradition, but transforms it into innovation.

Definition of SMEs in Europe		
Category:	Employees:	Turnover:
Medium Company	< 250	< 50 million Euro
Small Company	< 50	< 10 million Euro
Micro Company	< 10	< 2 million Euro

From project management to system management	
Project Management	*System Management*
Players: Supplier, Company, Designer, Customer	New Players: From the Nature to the World Population
Fields: Market, Know-how, Technology, traditional innovation, single project approach	New fields: Crowd sourcing, co-design, design thinking, system, incremental innovation
Skills/tools: project, style, invention, technology, machineries, marketing	New skills/tools: empathy, values, language, storytelling,
Goals: turnover, new customers and markets, new production tools, new products and services	New goals: Communication, contamination, vision, strategy, perception, culture
Project + System = Design Management	

Design Management Keywords	
Awareness	Values, identity, perception
Contamination	Brand, tools, workplace, products, services, suppliers, customers, nature, people, community
Skills	Enhancement of the latent potentiality
Technology	Know-how shifting, crossing, hybridization
Informations	Cool hunting, analyze, sharing, create content, be active
Communication	Globalization, glocalization, storytelling
Vision and Mission	Design thinking, be unique

Design Management Actions	
Research	Self analysis, competitors, positioning, perception, trend, target, mood
Development	Mission, vision, resources, productivity, wellness, workplace, costs rationalization, innovative products/services, innovative market opportunities

Incremental Innovation and Design Management

TRADITIONAL INNOVATION

INCREMENTAL INNOVATION

PURE INNOVATION

TRADITIONAL DESIGN PROJECT

DESIGN MANAGEMENT

ACADEMIC RESEARCH

The positioning of incremental innovation is halfway between the traditional simplistic innovation and high performances required for pure innovation. The positioning of Design Management is halfway between the traditional design that screams to the market and the complexity of the excellence of academic research.

Product Design.

In the word of Design, concepts as style and invention are undoubtedly very important. It's also important, however, the need to emancipate the *Design* word, that is not invention at all costs, and not simply a question of style. Design is first of all project, method, industrial culture. An object can be defined *a design object* when it is the result of a deep research, when it is the result of an accurate creative work, made of stylistic choices, ergonomic interactions, engineering, optimization of production, market distribution and packaging, marketing and communication, life-cycle and repair procedures, recycling and end-life disposal.

During the project, it may happen that some processes are more effective than others, more strategic than others, better managed than others. You can have excellent results, discrete or bad, but what distinguishes a *design object* is the result of this complex but essential tool that is the *project*. To realize a good design project is needed an holistic mindset, multidisciplinary, culturally opened to contamination.

A *design object* resists temporary fashion moods and lasts a long time. May become useless because of the changing of some habits or technologies, but remain an icon of style, cleverness, a symbol of the correct approach to the project. My Masters, at different times and in different ways, of this approach to the project are L.M. Van Der Rohe, Bruno Munari, Dieter Rams, Jonathan Ive, Oki Sato.

Then there are millions of commercial items on the shelves of shops and showrooms attracting people attention with an appealing style or functional inventions seemingly sensational. These products are often with a short life, because of fashion's language changes, or due to an overload of features sometimes useless.

L.M.Van Der Rohe: Vila Tugendhat, 1930, Brno, CZ.

Vila Tugendhat is a perfect example of good design, typical of the approach *Less is more*. The architecture talks with the surrounding landscape, all objects and furniture are designed to be perfectly integrated with the spaces they occupy, the functions of home automation facilitate and make more intense the daily life in this house. It's 1930, but Van Der Rohe has already applied an holistic approach to the project.
http://www.tugendhat.eu/

Apple: iPod Shuffle

The head of the design department of Apple, Jonathan Ive, following the design approach of Dieter Rams and his 10 rules for good design, created, with the iPod mp3 music player, a perfect example of good design. In this product, all the details are carefully designed, from the interface with the user to materials, packaging and communication. The product fully reflects the philosophy of company Apple. http://www.apple.com

Swatch

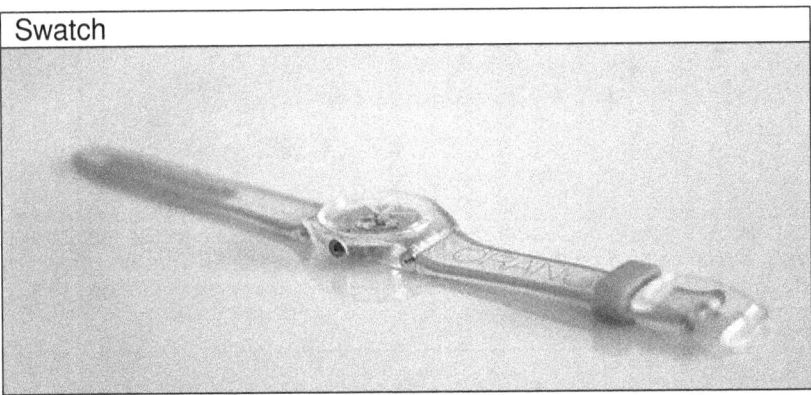

The Swatch watches are timeless products and can be used on all occasions. Another example of good design.
http://www.swatch.com

Nendo

Oki Sato is a young but established designer. His approach to the project is very emotional and philosophical. The product that comes from his project design is simple but timeless, tells a story and involves people in the atmosphere of the project.
http://www.nendo.jp/en/

Design Thinking.

Life is made up mainly of choices and decisions. Often we decide to stand still, not to choose, not to decide, transferring to others or to something else the weight of the consequences. I have learned, thanks to design, how fascinating is to get involved, choose, decide, research, understand and know. All this words, however, remains useless if you do not express your mind, body and soul, sharing and contaminating your ideas, if you do not use all your energy and passion to transform your ideas into actions, gestures, thoughts, objects, experiences. What matters is the will, the project that grows in your mind. Does not exist free time for a designer, says a friend. I agree with her. You have to project yourself everyday if you want to be the designer of you existence. Design is not a subject of study or business; is a lifestyle, is a mindset.

To make the *design thinking* become a useful state of mind, it takes a little of talent and a bit of commitment. It takes mental agility, wisdom, irony, sarcasm, and a lot of curiosity.
Knowing you do not know, as Socrates, the Athenian, said. However, even genius and recklessness, such as Socrates, the Brazilian footballer, who of freedom and

rebellion against the established patterns has made a way of life. Design Thinking is instinct, freedom of thought and expression, shamelessness, profanity, awareness, method. If you have a little bit of all these things then design thinking can do for you. The curriculum of study and business experiences that led me to write this text taught me to give equal importance to the great ideas and to the hard work. *Creativity meant nothing without method*, said the master Bruno Munari, and is summed up in these words the essence of the creative professions and design thinking.
Everything else is superficial style, unpredictable randomness and huge stroke of luck. The research in design projects is often underestimated, while it is in my opinion the decisive phase to give to ideas a solid foundation, to give innovative aspects and unexpected creative directions. Research is very important in design thinking methods. The times in which we live offers endless research resources, but like all tools at our disposal, is the way in which they are used to make a real difference. A design thinking approach should encourage natural instinct to know every thing that during a reading or a discussion proves unknown to you, and in this, respect than in the past, we have at our side the web and Wikipedia. However, is not enough.
A design thinking approach should encourage the passion for research, to link different concepts together, the ability of storytelling and the constancy in archiving cleverly all information collected during the research process.
A design thinking approach should also encourage working methods that stimulate the contamination, hybridization, but also a smart simplification of ideas. (Never forget the *Less is more* by L.M. Van Der Rohe). A clear and famous example of design thinking ap-

proach in design world is Fabio Novembre, a sort of demiurge more than a designer.
If you have talent, method, and a team of trusted employees who know their stuff, you can concentrate yourself at design thinking approach, and realize great design projects.

However, what is design? Explain what design is, it's becoming increasingly difficult, especially in Italy and Europe. The word *Design* is everywhere in any marketing campaign. The word *Design* has become part of the everyday vocabulary of all people, losing its original meaning of Project, becoming a definition that brings together some mainstream characteristics: cool, cute, modern, technologically advanced.
We, designers, have spent a lot of years to impose the importance of our role in society, industry and economy, and that's how we are rewarded.
We transformed ourselves into spirits of modern consumerism but we are compared by common people to artists or inventors. No one among the common people have a clear idea of what it really means to be a Designer and what Design means. Is that a fault of the companies and marketing departments that use the Design word for cheat people? Or it's a fault of the common people who have no culture and is easily duped? Definitely, but only partially. Designers have also a big responsibility, a fault of designers is to have invested too little in the future, focusing on the present. It is also a fault of trade associations and public institutions that remained obtuse, too aristocratic and self-referential. What can we do now to go back to the profound value of words Design and Designer? Hard to say. Someone with the gift of doing, tries to escape from this situation becoming a Maker, others, with the gift of storytelling, are rising to the rank of artists. Good escape routes, but the problem remains. Design,

Designer: we have to find other words or are we still in time to save them? We did not so much to solve this problem, but fortunately the crisisof this beginning of millennium has come to us for help. From compulsive consumerism we are moving inexorably to conscious consumerism, and something in the purchase, slowly, is changing.
Design, after all, is just that: awareness.

Design and Design Thinking approach are necessary practices to create something good, regardless of the field of application. Designer is a professional who knows the processes needed to achieve this goal, with the right approach of mindset. In design, as in other worlds, there are many nuances, but the essence is this: do something good, really good, to be available to the market.
If you ask me what are *Performing Arts* I can answer that are cinema, theater, are the mime on the street, are my cousin that marks the poetry for Christmas. But are also set design, script, costumes, vulgarity and sincere feelings, poetry. Even the arts, after all, would not exist without the workshops, galleries, dealers, museums, are made of poor lovers and rich people with bad taste.
We must get used to the idea that the new design is as varied as all other forms of expression. There is no rule to define what is right and what is wrong, what is design and what is not . We, designer, must be more aware, more careful, less superficial, less and less bigots. Let's get used to the idea that the design is made of everything, of people and objects, places and emptiness, blood and flesh, emotions and shit.

Design Thinking: we have this tool to try to change the world. Surely it is an utopia, but thanks to this utopia, we can try to do things better.

Milan Design Week , 2013

Wat is it? is design? is it art? neither of these things?

Elena Cadic

Design thinking is a mindset, a philosophy of life, not just a technical design tool. This necklace made of pencils is a creation by Elena Cadic. This object tells a story, expresses a philosophy, gives emotions. A good example of design thinking approach.

Creative tools.

There are different ways of being a designer. You can be, for example, a great technical designer, but having not the right awareness for creative tools. Or you can be a great creative designer, prepared to use the best tools of creativity, but not so good in production details and product engineering. It is not a matter of comparisons or rankings. Being an excellent technical designer is different from being a great creative designer. For a good project of Design Management we need both figures, but the creative designer is crucial in the developing of holistic systems.

Creative designer, thanks to design thinking approach, is the right player for Design Management projects. How to recognize a creative designer? How I recognize in myself a creative designer?

A creative designer must have three basic qualities: passion, curiosity, perseverance.
Passion: to be a creative designer is not a job, is a lifestyle. If you often confuse your being a person with your being professional, you are in the good way.
If on Saturday night, at a pizzeria with friends, the first thing you look at are the welded points of a stool, the effect to touch the wood of the bar and the font with which it is written the menu, before you even

think about your pizza and beer, then maybe you are in the good way.

Curiosity: being a designer means being a little artist, a little inventor, a little engineer, a little architect, a little graphic, a little photographer, a bit stylist, a bit commercial agent, a bit metalworker, a bit carpenter, a bit philosopher, a bit sociologist, a bit psychologist... at the same time you are nothing of these things and if you ever had a doubt to be really good at one of those things, it means that you are no longer thinking as a designer. Only if you have a lot of curiosity, the desire to touch, read, see, travel, only if you are willing to continuously learn and if you are aware that you'll never know enough about things, then you have the right mindset for a creative designer.

Perseverance: because to be a great creative designer is like trying to become a famous football player. One in a thousand makes it, and it is not just a matter of luck. In this business there is never rests, there are no weekends, you cannot be sick and you will never retire.

A good exercise for creative designers is to take pictures with mobile phone at all the things that intrigue you and you meet during the day.

Once a week, take a notebook and a pen and draw, take notes about what you were intrigued by, add notes about anything else you can think of, transcribe phrases, poems or quotations from movies and magazine, clippings sticks, pieces of objects that remind you particular materials and sensations.

If, after a month of this exercise, you're still taken pictures and you're still wasting your time cropping magazines, then probably you are the right guy for a creative design approach.

abitudinicreative

Collage is my favorite technique to create connections.

abitudinicreative

The world around us is a fundamental source of ideas and information. Taking pictures of all things that intrigue you and organize them into an archive is a powerful creative tool for your future projects.

**Design Management.
Protagonists and interlocutors.**

The two key figures for the management of creative projects and design management in a company are the entrepreneur and the designer.
In order to discuss about design management in SMEs is therefore essential to underline that the small entrepreneur is not a barbarian owner of a SUV that knows only blind work 24 hours a day, and a designer is not just an artist who designs cool business cards and sometimes creates miraculous innovations.
Similarly it must be underlined that only open minded entrepreneurs and designers can think of putting together their forces to deal with the challenges of the new millennium .
Thanks to my experience on both sides of the river, I will try with this text to stimulate more constructive cooperation between entrepreneurship and creativity.
Entrepreneur often focuses not only on profit, but also on self-assertion and on developing specific skills and self character.
Far from the typical alienation of employees, entrepreneur is able to concentrate passion and efforts with significant results both from a technical and commercial point of view .

As a result, especially for the older generation of entrepreneurs, SMEs accumulate invaluable knowledge resources concentrated in a single person.
The efforts dedicated to their own business are maximums, but are not accompanied by a willingness to share experience.
Another limit of SMEs organization is the consolidated operating processes.
Once reached a good profit and satisfied professional achievement, the entrepreneur finds himself in the position of not having the need to verify the efficiency of the processes and the management of the company.
As a consequence, the management of the company is based on experience and habits.
This type of management has zero impact from the point of view of investment, so the entrepreneur unconsciously is reassured about the quality of the management. The company operate with a mechanism that can ensure a good standard, but that does not exploit the full potential .
Even in cases of entrepreneurs particularly active in investments, often the resources are dedicated to the modernization and rationalization of traditional processes and traditional production or machineries.
More rare the cases where substantial part of the investment is dedicated to the research and development of alternative processes .
Generally in SMEs we find a good the propensity to do things, but a small propensity to plan and project.
SMEs have to understand that research and development are tools that can help companies to be more competitive, thanks to the analysis of incremental innovation projects and development of the system management.
From this approach derives an added value not only for the company but also for the community, which does not disperse knowledge, currently monopolized

by the mind and the hands of the entrepreneur, making it more accessible to everyone.
This management approach becomes an added value for the entrepreneur that enhances the unique capabilities of the organization, facilitating the solution of the most critical processes, such as the generational change.
The generational change is historically one of the most delicate phases for SMEs.
The need for continuity is not only economically and financially, are in addition to the need of operational continuity and know-how trasfer.
An adequate methodological attitude and a good design management project can minimize the risks in these sensitive stages of the company.

A planned management of the company also provides an extra opportunity for the designer who, thanks to its heterogeneous formation, can be one of the interlocutors of greater importance for SMEs development.
Designer, thanks to his natural propensity to the project, can assist the entrepreneur in the verification of the present situation and in the development of innovative activities, with the possibility to find new ways of propulsion to the company.
As noted above, for a fruitful collaboration between the two protagonists, it is imperative that next to the enlightened management of the entrepreneur there must be a conscious and responsible design management approach by the designer, who must give precedence to the reasons for the good project respect to the devotion of its creative egoism.
In addition, for a young designer, working for SMEs is a good opportunity to acquire technical and management information.
Compared to other kind of collaborations, the collaboration with SMEs makes possible to follow many fields

of design, from corporate communication to the design of industrial products or services.
All this experience is done without filters, in fact the designer in SMEs is in direct contact with the entrepreneur, the employees and the technicians.
Nevertheless, it is important to point out what an experience of this kind must keep away from creative alienation, typical of larger and more complex projects, for which designers often face defined segments, without being able to make experience of the overall project.
For young designers working with a small company should therefore be judged as indispensable opportunity to express themselves in many different fields, to test their skills and talents.
The designer have to organize the work to meet the needs of the company, giving further evidence of a propensity to design thinking.
Is instead responsibility of the entrepreneur to give free access to the potentialities and resources of knowledge of the company to the designer.

In addition to these two main protagonists, entrepreneur and designer, we have a lot of secondary characters, not less important for the success of the project, as suppliers, workers, employees, customers, and, more generally, anyone who can give new ideas for the design management project.

**Design Management.
Tools.**

The essential tools for a good design management project in SMEs are language, culture, technique and method.
The prerequisite for a good project relationship between entrepreneur and designer is the sharing of a common language.
Very often a collaboration can have problems due to the inability to communicate.
The language is made of words, gestures, signs, drawings and much more. It is important to clarify the basis of the project prior to incurring on dangerous misunderstandings.
The designer must have as a priority once again the success of the project with respect to the redundant personal affirmation.
If during the project development is necessary to use too often interpretations or translations, you have to change the language to greatly speed up the transmission of information, without compromising the quality and timing of implementation of the project.
It is important to adopt a common language, and from that base, grow together, entrepreneur and designer.
Therefore, it is important to use language not as a

weapon of oppression, rather to communicate well, quickly, without misunderstandings.
Examples of misunderstandings that waste much time are the use of different units of measurement between the designer and entrepreneur, millimeters versus centimeters, or the range of Pantone colors in contrast to the RAL range.
To choose the right mutual language to be adopted for a project may seem like a waste of time, but you will earn a lot of productivity during the project thanks to that.

Culture is a tool generally used with greater mastery by the designer, while the technical knowledge is an instrument generally used with greater mastery by the entrepreneur.
The instrument of the method have to be part of the experience both of the designer and the entrepreneur. For the designer the method is generally dictated by education and formation, for the entrepreneur by the experience.
Melt together training and experience, culture and technology, returns a powerful methodological tool that enriches both designer and entrepreneur, and also inevitably enriches the project itself, above all it gives added value to those who will benefit of the product or service: the customer.

The best way to add value to language, culture, technique and method, is to share experience.

Speaking of the cultural tool, we can simplify by saying that the designer must have good command of all that is expressive instrument, both historically and in contemporary times.
The study of expressive instruments such as art, graphics, cinema, photography, music, etc. must be

accompanied by a deep curiosity of the contemporary world and society and the essential knowledge of the history of design as necessary elements of comparison.
It may also be important to cultivate interest and curiosity for disciplines such as sociology, psychology, philosophy, etc.
Curiosity is therefore very important in the cultural education of a young designer or entrepreneur.

An essential cultural tool is without a doubt internet. The web allows us to stay connected with the daily life of thousands of people around the world. A young designer needs to have a deep understanding of social phenomena that surround it, of general mainstream cultures, all accompanied by a critical spirit.

Many companies, of all sizes, are too often engaged in traditional marketing projects and do not see the new things that are emerging in society. The young designer, well trained in design thinking and culturally dynamic, can filter this information, analyzing and storing to make them easily accessible to all company staff. The entrepreneur must be aware of the importance of the designer research works, not conditioned by the consolidated dynamics of the company. The culture of the designer is also essential to avoid redundancy and stylistic contradictions, to encourage consistency between the company identity and the product. In addition, in this case the task of the designer is to filter.

The experience is precious and must be defended, the know-how is an integral part of the company's value and must be preserved, but in SMEs, experience and know-how are too often useful only to the contingent needs, are not real resources for development.

Good entrepreneur should have the foresight to understand that sharing experience can be important for the growth of the company competitiveness.
Share experience does not mean to give away strategic information of the company, but give the opportunity to the designer to access to a basic knowledge of technical terminology, materials, manufacturing procedures, machinery, purchasing management, commercial structures.
Too often technical and business experience are managed directly by the entrepreneur, without being documented.

This way of managing know-how is anachronistic. Without having to formally certify the processes of managing the company, it is nevertheless essential to put in writing the business dynamics, even in a schematic way, to ensure an important investment in the future for the company.
Again, the keyword is to share. With simple initiatives such as making a small company handbook, the company experience is transformed from sterile knowledge applied to the daily needs in fruitful opportunity for company growth.

There is another fundamental element in a design management project: the method.

There are many schools of thought and many different approaches to design methods, many of which are equally valid.
The *right method* is often influenced by people and professionals participating in a project. We can certainly say that the holistic design thinking approach is the only attitude that can lead to a quality result.

**Design Management.
Methods.**

My approach to the method, basically born from the experience as an entrepreneur in my company, from project management in the field of ISO9000 and from the didactic structure of my educational curriculum as creative designer.
Planning a Design Management project, is often considered as a penance rather than as a resource.
The desire to get to work quickly or to get to a result in a hurry without having identified a method of approach to the project, ends in most cases with incomplete, common or redundant results.
A good design management project needs three steps: research, development, realization.

These three stages are the backbone of a good design method. I can testify from personal experience that especially in the micro companies these three steps are rarely used systematically.
For a number of reasons the step that most of all is shamefully abandoned is the research. In fact, the research step is often the crucial phase for a good design management result.
Sometime boring for the designer and at first glance unproductive for the entrepreneur, research is the

fundamental basis on which to build a solid design management project.

A project at the end can be good or bad for many reasons, difficult to predict certainty. However, when a project tells a story, certainly has many more weapons to be successful. Objects, people, places, if full of stories to tell, are extremely interesting. This is the power of storytelling.
Although our project is subject to this rule and the best way to tell a story is to dedicate time to a deep research. Technical research must be combined with a research driven by curiosity.
We need to gather more information as possible about our company, ask questions about the world around it and everything that can enrich the project.
All this information must be managed in a critical way, the task of the designer is to give an added value to research from the social and cultural point of view, the task of the entrepreneur is to promote research and give technical and technological tools to do it in the best way.

Thanks to this first step we have prepared the ground on which we will grow our ideas. To conclude our research process and start planting ideas, we need to define the unique characteristics of our project.
First of all to be able to tell a story with our project we need a name, a title. Therefore, we have to analyze all company aspects to add value to the project. The analysis of the human and technological resources of the company is an added value to our history, to our project.
Creative development of ideas is not exclusively romantic, anarchist and purely artistic, but also an highly professional and specific step.

At the same time the creative development process must maintain a profound narrative connotation, in continuity with the project, in order to continue the storytelling of our ideas with consistency.
The creative development of the project consists first of all in an exploratory phase of many different design directions, both rational and dreamlike.
In with this phase of the dreamlike sessions and streams of consciousness, you can go anywhere thanks to brainstorming techniques. We can adopt a method of logical relations between various premises going to conclusions in a network of relationship between every element born during the brainstorming. We can also create grids of icons, sketches or simplified prototypes, developing ideas and concepts.
These processes of creative development must always be subjected to some evaluation criteria, in order to simplify the synthesis of ideas.
The process of evaluation and validation of ideas is undoubtedly the most complex of the creative development step.

Entrepreneur and designer must put aside the instinct for protection against their own ideas, considering first the importance of a good design project.
The more people *contaminate* ideas in this creative development step, the more any single idea have opportunity to continue his journey with strength in the continuation of the project.

A contaminated idea is first an enriched idea.

What criteria are the best to select and summarize the most interesting ideas? It is a very difficult answer. Using a quote from Enzo Mari I can say that a project must involve a change, of whatever nature. So, select the ideas that most enrich what you started from.

Making this selection, never forget that should be consistent with the story you're telling.
At this point there is nothing left to do but to submit to the client or market the synthesis of the project.

We are at realization step.

For the success of the project it is important that all aspects reflect the designed storytelling.
The result will be not a redundant re-styling, but a real project, in the literal sense, with deep technical and poetic values.
The result of a good Design Management project is not simply a new product to sell, but a new point of view for the company, a new system made of business and people, made of design, production, organization, communication and marketing.

All this new resources will help the company to be more competitive, to improve the brand perception by the market, to improve the brand awareness by the employees and suppliers, will help to manage every future single project with more power and effectiveness.

**Design Management.
Brand Awareness and Identity.**

The greatest dangers for the brand identity of SMEs are essentially two.
The first is to tell what you are not, lying more or less consciously, the second danger is to be identified for something that you are not.
Distracted by habits, the entrepreneur may not realize that his company is not perceived in the right way from the outside, occasionally causing simply confusion, in other cases causing business problems.

In the evaluation of design processes we often talked about sharing as main keyword. In brand analysis the main keyword is consistency.
Many small importers are masked behind a picture of manufacturers. This corporate image management may make sense today exclusively for speculative purposes, but has no long-lasting result for those who really wanted to enhance their own business.
The market is much more mature, the economic crisis pushes, at all levels, to purchase in a more reflective and conscious way.
SMEs have to simply appear as they are.

Obviously, you need to take full advantage of company features. To do so, first you need to identify the potential and limits of the company.
Very often, thanks to young designer attitude, not yet affected by the dynamics of the market, you can transform many limitations of your company into opportunities.
Note that are strengths and weaknesses to make us unique and interesting, not a mask of perfection.
The entrepreneur have to be bothered by a renewal operation of its company image, as long as this is the result of a planned project and not a mere exercise in style.
SMEs, apart from very rare cases, it is not able to impose itself as trend setter, does not have the necessary resources to establish itself as a protagonist, but is forced to be a follower.
Every company, no matter how small, has its own identity, it has character, it has habits, has a history, has desires. Collect this information and translate them into a coherent corporate image provides opportunities for business opportunities often unexpected.
The goal is to tell a story about the identity of our company, through the logo, through the organization, the workplace, the advertising material.
Everything must be consistent, honest.

A good brand design project have to consider also the awareness of the values of the brand by suppliers, employees, external collaborators.
This is very important to give more power at the company to be competitive and well organized.

**Design Management.
Corporate structure.**

SMEs services or products are offered to the market often in a very conservative way or with an attitude too related to the fashion mood of the moment.

Many SMEs have latent potential that the habit to a traditional industrial process fails to emerge.
With the help of the designer, the company can enhance the consolidated production processes with incremental innovation projects that help to be more competitive.
The entrepreneur, often engaged in many activities, it's not always able to understand the latent potential of the company.
The designer have to manage the evaluation of the corporate structure with design methodology, putting in practice the three basic steps: research, development, realization.
First, you should make a map of the responsibilities, duties and skills. Who decides what? Who does what? Moreover, what preparation or aptitude is related to that role or that responsibility? Another key is mapping the resources of technology and production machineries of the company. Machines, mechanical tools, molds, equipments. The designer must also collect in-

formation on what goes before and what comes after the corporate system, a careful evaluation of the suppliers and market.
The next step is to identify the main procedures for core activities of the company.
Prepare brief specifications containing the most important aspects of the relationship with strategic suppliers allows you to avoid misunderstandings. For the same reason, also the analysis of internal activities, if handled systematically with a project attitude, can optimize time and resources, for instance by adopting a procedure for order receipt, order confirmation, sales and post-sales activities, customer satisfaction monitoring.
Equally important is a systematic management of procedures for the creation of a product, from design to production, to shipping for sale.
In product design projects is important to take into account all the aspects of the life of a product, so easily the end customer will have the perception to have purchased a designed product, and therefore a product of true design.
The design of a product , not to be a simple exercise in style, have to concentrate the corporate philosophy, the exploitation of the potential of strategic suppliers, the development of human and technology potential, the internal and external logistics, the packaging, handling and shipping, the response to market demands and the reports from customers.

It's also important to define responsibilities and resources, underline requirements of the projects, the main project processes and the results evaluation.
With a correct attitude of design management you can have a better corporate structure and better products.

**Design Management.
Be known and be informed.**

Communication and information are essential tools for SMEs to stay competitive in the market. Thanks to modern technology, communication and information can be managed independently by the company.
To optimize the potential of tools such as the internet, the intervention of a designer is desirable, as the corporate image of the company is so much more effective if it is consistent and coordinated.
Consistency is therefore the keyword to communicate with success and must be accompanied by a systematic propensity to the storytelling. Generate emotions through the storytelling allows you to enter deeply into the psychology of those who read or listen to us. Everything that comes out of our company should therefore be consistent and tell emotions.
Thanks to the web it is always easier to communicate at the same time it is always easier to stay in the shadows. The website is a virtual storefront, almost at zero cost, but at the same time, because of the ease access to this tool, is easier to remain invisible if it is not utilized properly.
A website that stay anonymous, immobile and inconsistent with the company's image can then be useless, if not counterproductive. The website should therefore be designed and be the result of research, development, realization processes.

Storytelling, intrigue and be yourself are the weapons at our disposal for an effective communication. The designer has technical and cultural tools to better manage this kind of projects.
Internet is not only a place of communication, but also of information, in a continuous contact with the reality that surrounds us, with the market, with the competitors. SMEs, even more than large industrial companies, can evolve through a continuous and systematic approach to research on the internet, visiting fairs and cultivating the reading and analysis of magazines. The management of a small organized archive of information obtained from the Internet can be an interesting activity to support creative projects.

Be informed about the world and the market is a strategic activity that can give important opportunities to be more competitive.

**Design Management.
Foresight and storytelling.**

Ensure continuity and future at company results in SMEs means first of all to manage loyalty and training. Using these two keywords our propensity to the future can be perceived positively, by company organization and by the market.
Meet the needs and expectations of the customer must be considered a fundamental tool for the growth of the company.
The management of the customer have to be planned and formalized, with the use of specific documentation, with specific procedures, with the systematic collection of information about customer satisfaction.
The collaboration of the designer in this processes can be an opportunity.
In addition, the management of the relationship with the client is in fact a process in which creativity, if used consistently, can give unexpected fruits. Organizing an event of contact between company and customer, realize smart communication using internet, plan campaigns to collect information on customer satisfaction. All of these actions, if handled with particular attention to corporate philosophy, can return important results: the dissemination of information through word of mouth thanks to customers, a power-

ful form of advertising at no cost, the collection of information, useful to reconstruct a profile of our target in the market.

These actions to be truly incisive must be designed, must include planning and creativity. The collaboration between designer and entrepreneur is a strategic element of consolidation and revitalization of SMEs.

An important tool of relationship between the company and the outside world is the sharing of knowledge.

Always within the limits of respect for privacy and the protection of its assets, the sharing of information is an opportunity of contact with suppliers and customers, which can help giving ideas to simplify some business processes, minimize misunderstandings and drastically cut the inefficiency in production.

In a word, you could say that even in SMEs is necessary to make culture.

If culture management is then characterized by creative values, can be a very important opportunity for communication, which gives added value to company image.

The most powerful weapon is the creation of a sense of belonging. Involving suppliers and customers in our projects is undoubtedly a process with a high innovative coefficient, culturally and educationally.

Training courses for entrepreneur and employees allow further impetus to the activity of the company.

To build effective training actions, we also need method, all educational activity must be designed and planned to be part of the design management project.

Emme Italia factory

The value of a company is often calculated only numerically. We calculate turnover, real estate properties, industrial machineries etc. That is correct, but not enough. The value of a company is increasingly linked to the value of its brand and the value of the company management. Design management is the tool that helps us to give value to our company and to make us more competitive. Design Management is a tool that works in quantity and quality.

DME Award

DME Award is an event to valorise design management in European companies. The questionnaires for the assessment of **DME AWARD** are very useful tools to monitor the situation in your company and evaluate improvements.
http://www.designmanagementeurope.com

Workplace Design.

We spend a lot of time in our workplace. Designing these places in an innovative way allows us to improve the lives of many people.
The systemic crisis that we are experiencing gives us the ability to imagine new horizons, to give space to a different idea of professional achievement. Culture, contamination, quality of relationships, enhancement of responsibility, harmony of space, an idea of the future that will help us live better.

A workplace is made also of cultural processes. Designing relations mean to help more productive relations between people who share a workspace . The profound significance of this process is mainly cultural. The office space is too often a transposition on the desk of the industrial assembly line. Productivity is measured almost exclusively quantitatively and not qualitatively.
The worker is often brought to evaluate a workplace for earning potential and career opportunities, not for the enrichment of culture and personal well being.
However, there are different ways to think about job and workplace. Adriano Olivetti was a pioneer in that field.
His business idea was born in the 50s of the last century but is still surprisingly us. In the last 60 years,

unfortunately, the only business target was the logic of profit. The global crisis that we are experiencing could be the driving force to revive the hypothesis of a different future, as it was for the Olivetti the *tabula rasa* after the second world war.

To design a creative office the first challenge then is to find solutions to stimulate relations, cultural growth and employees well-being.
To stimulate relations between individuals we must deeply analyze the protagonists of the working environment and identify ways of contamination.
The workplace is the container of the relationships between individuals, not only a physical container but also and perhaps especially a social place. The first study to be carried out is therefore the barriers that limit the social and cultural contamination in the workplace.
Solutions to these needs of contamination are for example the creation of spaces for sharing activities outside of work time. However, we must not limit ourselves to think only about a gym or a library, these solutions are certainly interesting, but superficial, we must think about more immersive group experiences. Create, for example, laboratories between parents and children, specialized educators and families. If you are a micro company and your are too small to afford such services, break through the inertia and think of an integrated program with other micro companies. Only through cultural and social challenges we can really boost the relations between individuals.

The most important initiatives to stimulate cultural growth is undoubtedly the sharing of knowledge.
It's important for SMEs to share experiences, content and professionalism. Being jealous of our knowledge

does not pay. Have a blog, organize meetings and workshops.
Too often this type of initiatives are only seen as self-promotion moments. The goal instead should not be commercial, but cultural. A change of perspective often difficult to explain to the entrepreneur, but crucial to obtain benefits, also commercial benefits, in the medium and long term.

For the wellbeing of employees is important to enhance the unique characteristics of any individual to increase the productivity and the involvement in the design management project.
It is also important to think about spaces and initiatives that satisfy the natural inclination of every human to individuality.
Introducing a workplace corporate system that prioritises the quality of working life improves the social dynamics of the company and makes the company very attractive, facilitating the inclusion of great professional profiles.

Too often in SMEs the word *leadership* is confused with the word *arrogance*.
To think for SMEs only about a pyramidal organization system is anachronistic, companies that still use only this system will not have an easy life in the near future. Responsibilities and competencies are much more fluid, to be important is company network and connections between people, not the steps of authority.
The traditional office layout (presidential office, executive office, operative office etc.) is just the consequence of an old idea of workplace organization.
An innovative workplace design should take into account the need for a more fluid network of people, the need for teamwork and individual work.

Individuality, sharing and contamination are the key words that allow employees to grow together, be more productive and happy.
At first glance you might think of a utopian vision of the workplace, but we have numerous examples of international companies that had important benefits from having implemented innovative policies of internal organization and creative office layout.
With pyramidal systems we have frequent phenomena of envy and jealousy.
This change of perspective, from vertical to network, create an innovative office environment that gives value to the brand.

A workplace is obviously characterized also by architectural aspects. A good workplace design project, as we have seen, must contain first cultural and social innovation.
From this premise it is possible to develop an architectural and interior design project truly innovative. Architecture and interior design allow us to give substance to the innovations previously assumed.
The harmony of the structures, environments and objects that surround us greatly increase the success of a design management project.

For an innovative workplace design project, we have to go beyond the traditional ideas of office layout and office spaces. For example, traditionally the reception space is a cold business card without emotions. Sometimes we can find receptions with exhibition spaces or conversation areas. Can we go further? We can imagine to organize events and share culture, organize training events, sharing services (wi-fi connection, library, coffee corner) not only with our selected customers and employees but also with the community.

Reception not as an instrument of persuasion but as an opportunity for sharing culture and a tool of contamination for our ideas.

A Workplace Design project is not simply an architectural draw and a selection of office furniture, is first of all a social and cohabitation project, is thinking about the wellness of any individuals.
For this reason the best way to get important information for our workplace design project is to ask employees what they like. The Workplace Design project have to be a synthesis of the company's needs, the needs of workers, the needs of community, the brand values and the vision of the company.

Milan Design Week, 2013.

Architecture is only one aspect of a project of Workplace Design. Architecture is the finalization of a complex project that also has social and philosophical aspects.

Milan Design Week, 2012.

Interior Design is not simply a selection of office furniture. Interior design is the tool that we need to put employees in right relationship. Each person must have their own individual space and must have the possibility to easily share the work with others. In addition, the company itself must have exclusive spaces and inclusive spaces, spaces dedicated to the business activities and spaces opened to the community.

Strategic Design.

The biggest mistake of many SMEs is to be too focused on what is happening today, without projecting a vision of the company in the future.
Foresight is the key word to give competitiveness to our company not only now, but also in the near future.

The short-term tactical actions are good, but they must be integrated in a strategic project that have a medium-long term view.

Even in the strategic design we have three basic steps: research, analysis, realization.

During the research phase you should check the trend of your specific business sector (cool hunting) and the trends of the areas close to yours. This second research is crucial to have fresh information, not conditioned by your sector habits.
All material must be cataloged, in particular images and annotations about the values and styles that the market demands. We have also to make a research about values of our company. Research must be done using images, annotations, objects, materials, music, movies, books, food, places etc. We must collect information on our trading partners, our suppliers, our

competitors. All this information has to be analyzed in strategic projection.

Research material must be analyzed and must be measured the characteristics of the brand, our strengths and our weaknesses, must be created a map with a clear positioning of our brand and our competitors.

Finally, all the information obtained should be used to build a plan of action, underlining brand values and indicating the goals we want to achieve, both quantitative and qualitative.

Strategic design is the GPS that helps us to plan the future of our Design Management project.

SID Design Workshop. Map of keywords.

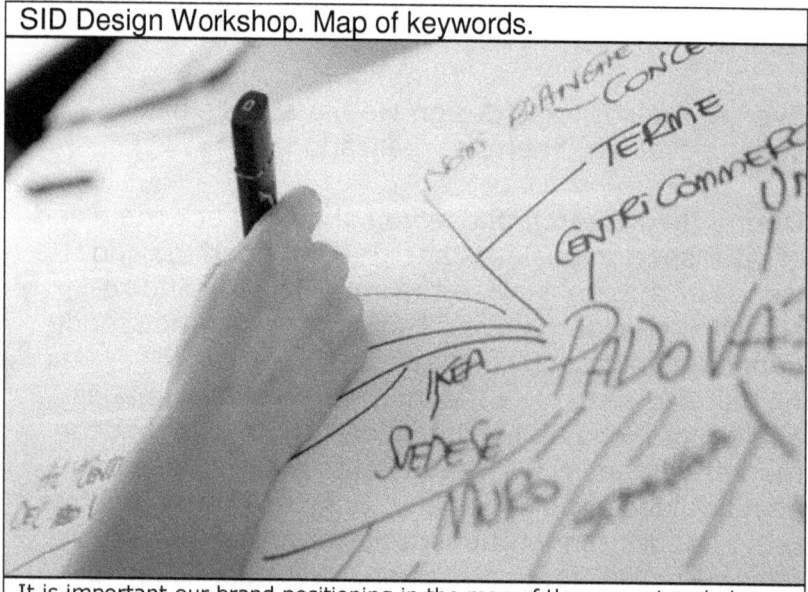

It is important our brand positioning in the map of the present and plan our journey to the future.
http://scuolaitalianadesign.com/

Brand reputation, web and social networks.

Many SMEs and entrepreneurs have a very depressing way to approach the web and marketing on the web. Someone has the fear of losing its status of serious company, someone has the fear of negative feedback from customers, or terrified of targeted attacks in the shadows of the web by competitors.
Someone else has the conviction that the easily access to a large number of users on the web is a huge opportunity to make money quickly.
Of course, the web is a dangerous place and it is also a place that facilitates very much the business, but the secret for a good project of web marketing have to be first of all a good project.
With a good web marketing project the brand can receive from a lot of ideas, constructive criticism, new contacts, visibility.
If a brand uses the web and social networks properly, stimulating discussion and enriching with interesting content the brand communication, in the long run will build a brand perception and a brand reputation of inestimable value, unthinkable before the era of web and social networks.

Once again, the difference is the culture and the quality of the marketing project. In social networks in particular, often the banal content, repetitive and self-referential is immediately transformed into garbage, the good contents into business opportunities.

The massive marketing is not wrong in itself, but must be well done. The web offers us many opportunities for quality marketing, that is really a shame to focus only on quantity and profit.
The risk of superficial marketing campaigns is wasting energy if not to jeopardize our brand reputation.
The main difference with a good web marketing campaign is essentially the perspective.
A good web marketing campaign is made of tactical actions for brand visibility in the short term and strategic actions looking for brand reputation in long term.
There is nothing more important, especially in the web era, than a respectable reputation and a network of influential contacts.
Making quality web marketing means having foresight, method and culture. You do not need huge economic resources, you need patience, time, energy, mindset.

Work on brand reputation not necessarily mean to be too serious. You can also be cute and funny, but always with the class and elegance.
Always think about your brand in the web e in the social networks with a bit of understatement.

Corporate social responsibility.

Corporate Social Responsibility is an important topic inside a Design Management project. Thanks to a new, more conscious approach to consumerism by customers, Corporate Social Responsibility it is increasingly important for a company.
Particularly in times of crisis like the one we are going through, those who have had more in the past should feel the need to reallocate some resources to community.
If anything in this field moves, the merit is often not because of big companies, but because of SMEs.
I had the pleasure of meeting recently a lot of interesting small projects of good marketing that impressed me positively, bringing together business, profit, entrepreneurship, craftsmanship, education, nature, charity.
SMEs cannot do miracles for social projects, and all businesses, even the smallest ones, exist in the first place to create profit.
However, there are several ways to invest in your brand reputation and marketing. Some are tactically effective only in the short term. Other, more culturally

complex, are strategically designed to give interesting results in the medium and long term.
Corporate Social Responsibility is a serious and difficult matter, but there are many small useful things to do, thanks to a good marketing approach.

Socially useful projects must be integrated into Design Management project in order to ensure the greater effectiveness. These initiatives must not be shouted, do not have to be a clever way to attract attention and make profit, must be in line with company's values and must be an integral part of the entrepreneur culture and mindset.

Monte Zovo Winery, 2013.

Industrial activities must respect environment and nature. If your business is an example of excellence in this field, it is right to communicate this to the market with targeted marketing actions.

The future is now.

A recent study by University of Phoenix says that the most important drivers of change in the next ten years will be the longevity of the population, the increase in smart technologies, the increase in computational power of computers, a new balance between mass media, the increase of the collective intelligence, the increase in connectivity between individuals.
This situation will cause a change in the demand for work skills of people and companies.
In 2020 work skills like sense making, social intelligence, adaptive and design thinking, cross-cultural competency, computational thinking, new media competency, transdisciplinarity, virtual team building, will become increasingly important.

We can prepare ourselves and our companies for this journey into the future by applying the best tools we have available.
Between all available tools, Design Management is probably the most important for SMEs.

We build a better future with everyday actions.
The future is now, welcome to the future.

Venice Architecture Biennale, 2010.
The future is now, welcome to the future.

Bibliography and sitography.

- Bruno Munari, *Da cosa nasce cosa*, Ed. Laterza, 1981
- V.Vercelloni, *L'avventura del design: Gavina*, Ed. Jaca Book, 1987
- Lee McCormack, *Designers are wankers*, About Face, 2005
- Karim Rashid, *Design your self*, Harper Collins, 2006
- Gino Finizio, *Design & Management*, Skira, 2002
- Brigitte Borja de Mozota, *Design Management*, FrancoAngeli, 2008
- Enzo Mari, *Progetto e passione*, Ed.Bollati Boringhieri, 2001
- Naomi Klein, *No logo*, BUR, 2010
- Cabirio Cautela, *Strumenti di design management,* FrancoAngeli, 2007
- Arianna Vignati, *Design e competitività delle PMI,* Maggioli, 2009
- Stefano Micelli, *Futuro artigiano,* Marsilio, 2011
- Antonio Galdo, *L'egoismo è finito,* Einaudi, 2012
- Donald Norman, *The design of future things,* Basic Books, 2007
- Donald Norman, *Living with complexity,* Pearson, 2011
- Bassani e Sbalchiero, *Brand Design,* Alinea, 2002
- Sophie Lovell, *Dieter Rams: as little design as possible,* Phaidon, 2011
- Institute for the Future, *Future Work Skills 2020*, Un. of Phoenix, 2011
- Alessandro Barison, *Appunti di design management*, ed.lulu, 2011

- European Design Centre: www.edc.nl
- Design Management Europe: www.designmanagementeurope.com
- The free Encyclopedia: www.wikipedia.org

Thanks.

I want first of all to apologize for my English, I hope that is good enough to be easily understood.

I want then to thank all my friends that helped me in this project, and to thank all my readers.

About me.

ADIMEMBER

I am Alessandro Barison. I was born in 1976 in Padova, Italy, where I attended scientific studies. Afterwards I studied at the Scuola Italiana Design of Padova, where I earned a specialization in Creative Design. In 1997 I began my professional career in Emme Italia srl as sales manager and design manager. In 2009 I received the honourable mention for a design management project in a micro company at DME awards. In 2009 I also founded the design and innovation blog abitudinicreative.it. Since 2010 I'm ADI design member (Italian Industrial Design Association).

I collaborate as a consultant specialized in creative design and design management with various institutions such as Scuola Italiana Design, Université Paris Ouest Nanterre La Défense, Torino Design Week and others.

alessandro barison

www.ingramcontent.com/pod-product-compliance
Lightning Source LLC
Chambersburg PA
CBHW070425180526
45158CB00017B/768